SHAH 'ABBAS AND THE TREASURES
OF IMPERIAL IRAN

SHAH 'ABBAS

AND

THE TREASURES

OF

IMPERIAL IRAN

Sheila R. Canby

THE BRITISH MUSEUM PRESS

Half-title page and frontispiece: Details from prayer rug, Iran, late 16th to
early 17th century. See **34**, p. 63. Left: Detail from illuminated manuscript,
Bustan of Sa'di, Iran, late 15th century. See **30**, p. 58. Right: Details from
page from a collection of *ghazals*, or love poems, Iran, 1551. See **52**, p. 94.

Note on dates: The Muslim calendar starts in AD 622, the year of Muhammad's
hijra, or flight, from Mecca to Medina, which is why some precise dates are given
in the form of the AH (*anno hijri*) date followed by the Christian calendar date.

709.5509032 CAN

CONTENTS

Map   6

Introduction   8

Dandies and other denizens of Isfahan   18

Traders, travellers and envoys   36

Sufis and pilgrims   54

Royal artists and the new style   76

Further reading   95

Illustration acknowledgements   96

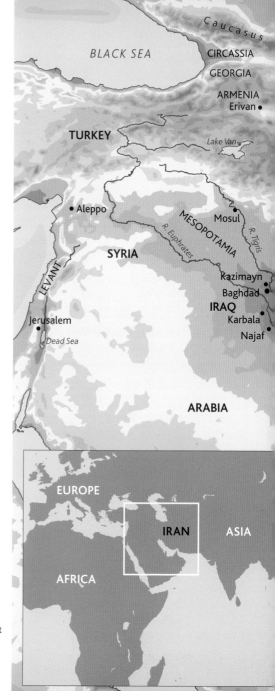

Map of Iran and the Near East

BARSARAN

TRANSOXIANA

CASPIAN SEA

ountains

ARABAGH

SHIRVAN

R. Oxus

Bukhara

TALISH

Julfa · Kalkhuran
· Ahar
Tabriz · Ardabil

AZERBAIJAN

TABARISTAN

GILAN

Farahabad

Ashraf

Nishapur · Mashhad

URDISTAN

Elburz Mountains

Qazvin

Tehran MAZANDARAN

KHURASAN

URISTAN

Zagros Mountains

Qum

Dasht-i-Kavir
Desert

IRAN

· Kashan

Jowshaqan

· Isfahan

Herat

AFGHANISTAN

KHUZISTAN

· Yazd

Dasht-i-Lut Desert

FARS

Basra

SISTAN

Kirman

Shiraz

PERSIAN
GULF

Bandar 'Abbas

BAHRAIN I.

HORMUZ I.

QISHM I.

MAKRAN

OMAN

N

0   500 miles

0   500 km

INTRODUCTION

Who was Shah ʿAbbas? Why is he the best-known king to have ruled Iran in the past five hundred years? What did he do to ensure the survival of his empire and the flowering of Iranian culture? In 1587, the first year of his reign, he was only sixteen years old, and the prospects for his success as a state-builder looked grim. The Ottoman Turks had occupied western Iran, the Caucasus and Iraq, and the Uzbeks controlled Khurasan, Iran's north-eastern province. Inside Iran, powerful tribes were vying with each other for military power and control over the new shah. The young shah needed a master plan to restore his country's political, economic and military fortunes. Luckily, his reign lasted for forty-two years, giving him time to transform Iranian society, build a new capital at Isfahan, replenish the national treasury and revive the country's religious institutions.

Four shahs from the Safavid dynasty preceded Shah ʿAbbas. The first, Ismaʿil I, came to power in 1501 and ruled from his capital at Tabriz in north-west Iran. The Safavids were descended from a mystic, or Sufi, called Shaykh Safi al-Din, who had established a dervish order at Ardabil, east of Tabriz near the Caspian Sea. As a result, Ismaʿil's supporters accepted the teachings of Shaykh Safi al-Din and considered Ismaʿil, as his heir, their spiritual master. When he became shah, Ismaʿil declared Shiism the state religion. This branch of Islam considers ʿAli ibn Abi Talib, the Prophet Muhammad's cousin and son-in-law, to be his rightful heir. Three of Muhammad's companions were appointed caliph, or successor,

1. Portrait of Shah ʿAbbas, attributed to Bishn Das, Mughal India, *c.*1618. Opaque watercolour and gold on paper, 18.1 × 9 cm.
In an age when diplomatic missions were a leisurely affair, the ambassador from the court of Jahangir, Emperor of Mughal India, spent six years, from 1613 until 1619, in Iran. In this likeness, the Indian artist Bishn Das captured the shrewd intelligence of the shah.

before 'Ali, so their partisans claimed that they represented the Sunna, or right path. The Shi'i followers of 'Ali consider him to be the First Imam, or infallible religious guide, followed by other Imams who were his descendants. The Safavids accepted Twelve Imams, the last one of whom disappeared in AD 873 and, it is believed, will return as a Mahdi, or Messiah, to establish the Shi'i dominion on earth. 'Ali and his grandson, Husayn, were both murdered by Sunnis, thus giving rise to a cult of martyrdom.

By pronouncing Iran a Shi'i realm, Shah Isma'il emphasized a national identity that was distinct from that of Iran's Sunni Ottoman and Uzbek neighbours. Thus, even though Isma'il himself, as a native of Azarbaijan, spoke Azari Turkish rather than Persian, his society would become rooted in a belief system that set it apart from earlier regimes and his enemies and that came to be recognized as particularly, though not exclusively, Iranian. Much of the reign of the next Safavid shah, Tahmasp (1524–76), was concerned with aligning Shi'i practice and Islamic law. To do this, Shah Tahmasp needed to control the same tribes that had brought his father to the throne. He decided to interject a new element into the higher echelons of Safavid society in order to dilute the tribes' power, promoting slaves from the Caucasus who were converts to Islam (*ghulam*s) to positions of responsibility in the royal household. When Shah 'Abbas ascended the throne, he adopted this policy wholeheartedly.

Under Shah Tahmasp, the arts of painting, calligraphy, carpet-weaving and textile manufacturing flourished. Although he constructed a new capital at Qazvin, north-west of Tehran, he did not commission any major mosques or other religious buildings. Rather, he added structures to existing complexes, such as a large domed chamber at his ancestral shrine at Ardabil. The luxurious objects that can be associated with Shah Tahmasp attest to his discerning taste and the distinctive pictorial and decorative style characteristic of his reign. During the chaotic reigns of his successors, Isma'il II (1576–7)

2. Maidan-i Naqsh-i Jahan, Isfahan.
This aerial view of the great maidan includes the congregational mosque, the Masjid-i Shah, in the foreground; the Mosque of Shaykh Lutfallah at the right; and the Ali Qapu palace at the left. Note how the façades of the mosques fall on the axis of the maidan while their prayer halls are angled in order to be oriented properly to Mecca.

and Muhammad Khudabandeh (1577–87), the artistic legacy of Shah Tahmasp remained fixed. No major royal buildings survive from this period, and patronage of painting and the book arts shifted to wealthy noblemen or Safavid royal women. While some royal women concentrated their patronage on Shi'i shrines, others supported the painters and calligraphers of their deceased husbands. Some artists adopted mannerist forms – attenuated, bending figures with elongated necks and small faces – but much of the pictorial art associated with Qazvin in this period lifelessly imitates work from the 1530s and 1540s, Shah Tahmasp's heyday as a patron.

Soon after Shah 'Abbas came to the throne, he reconstituted

the staff of the royal library. More than a repository of books, the library incorporated an artists' workshop, employing calligraphers, painters, bookbinders, illuminators and specialist assistants such as gilders, marblers, and glue- and paper-makers. These people not only produced illustrated manuscripts but also worked on single-page calligraphies or paintings for inclusion in albums, and supplied designs to workers in other media, such as ceramic tile-makers and weavers. Although large-scale architectural projects commissioned by Shah 'Abbas began to appear only in the second decade of his reign, production of manuscripts, paintings, drawings and calligraphy increased as soon he came to power.

From 1587 to 1598, Shah 'Abbas endeavoured to consolidate his control over Iran and regain territory lost to his enemies. He also began buying land in Isfahan, an ancient Iranian city which he visited on hunting expeditions. In 1598 he moved the capital from Qazvin to Isfahan and began to develop a royal precinct around an enormous plaza, the Maidan Naqsh-i Jahan, to be surrounded by an arcade containing shops. He also commissioned buildings on all four sides of the maidan. Thus, the multi-storey royal palace, the Ali Qapu, faced the shah's private mosque, later named the Mosque of Shaykh Lutfallah. At the southern end of the maidan, construction of a new congregational mosque began in 1612–13; it was still incomplete at the time of Shah 'Abbas's death in 1629. At the northern end, a monumental portal was built to lead into a new bazaar for luxury goods. In addition to the buildings centred on the maidan, a grand avenue with the palatial residences of Safavid grandees joined the part of Isfahan newly developed by Shah 'Abbas with a bridge to new southern suburbs. It was here, in 1604, that he resettled the population of the Armenian city of Julfa who had been displaced as a result of hostilities between Iran and Turkey.

The new buildings in Isfahan ordered by Shah 'Abbas demonstrate his determination to make his mark with impressive monuments

3. Archer, Isfahan, second half of the 17th century. Glazed tile, h. 16.5 cm. Hunting was the favourite pastime of Shah 'Abbas, a sport he enjoyed while travelling around his realm. Even before he moved his capital to Isfahan, he often visited the region on hunting expeditions. Although firearms had been in military use since the 16th century, Iranians were slow to replace swords and bows and arrows with guns for hunting.

showcasing a novel decorative style that would reflect the modernity and identity of his reign. The tiles that sheath the interior and exterior surfaces of the two mosques on the maidan incorporate floral and other decorative devices which also appear in the textiles, carpets and manuscript illumination of the period. In the Ali Qapu palace, wall paintings of Europeans and Iranians drinking wine or picnicking include private, secular imagery that would never have adorned a religious building. Meanwhile the façade of the monumental bazaar portal facing on the maidan included a large painting of a battle, an acceptable subject for a public structure.

In order to pay for his building campaigns and social programmes, Shah 'Abbas needed to stimulate the Iranian economy. One way of achieving this was to involve the Armenians of Isfahan in selling, and eventually producing, both raw and woven silk. The Armenians built on pre-existing trade networks in Europe and India to develop a thriving silk trade. With the silver that Europeans paid for these fabrics, Iran could continue to pay for the range of goods it bought from India. Along with his desire to open new markets in Europe, Shah 'Abbas welcomed Europeans to Isfahan. Their presence, along with the gamut of Middle Eastern and South Asian populations, was reflected in the saying 'Isfahan is half the world'.

Unlike his predecessors, Shah 'Abbas dealt ruthlessly with the Turkman tribes who had previously controlled the Safavid military, replacing their commanders with *ghulam*s. These men had been raised at the Safavid court and were loyal only to the shah. They helped him not only defeat his enemies and restore Iran's territory to its mid sixteenth-century boundaries but also disseminate the new style of art and design to the provinces.

One important aspect of the reign of Shah 'Abbas was his public display of piety through pilgrimage to important shrines. In 1608

4. Ali Qapu palace, Isfahan, *c.***1598–1612.** When Shah 'Abbas shifted the capital to Isfahan, he refurbished a pre-existing palace and renamed it Ali Qapu (visible at the right). Designed for administrative purposes and royal entertaining, the palace consists of six storeys with a platform on the third storey from which the shah and his guests could view entertainments in the maidan.

he announced a major donation of all his Chinese porcelains, Persian poetical and historical manuscripts, jades and other precious objects to his dynastic shrine at Ardabil. At the same time, he presented his Qur'ans and Arabic scientific texts to the Shrine of Imam Riza at Mashhad. A leading cleric had probably advised him on which Qur'ans and scientific manuscripts to give to the shrine at Mashhad, the most important Shi'i site in Iran, while his chief librarian and treasurer would have been instrumental in choosing the gifts for Ardabil. The items given to both shrines were all of the highest value and, as such, fitting donations. But they also represented the taste of the past, which Shah 'Abbas wished to supplant with a visual idiom of his own. The opulent silk and gold textiles and carpets, calligraphy and paintings produced for him embody the new style of Isfahan and show how the idea of what was valuable shifted from imported porcelains and old Qur'ans to a new class of treasures.

Following pages
5. Masjid-i Shah, Isfahan, 1612/13 – c.1630. This 'Mosque of the Shah' was the first congregational mosque constructed in Iran for more than a century. It includes two theological colleges and a vast central courtyard to accommodate large numbers of worshippers. Its decoration consists of dazzling blue and yellow tilework covering most of the interior spaces as well as the exterior façade and domes.

DANDIES AND OTHER DENIZENS OF ISFAHAN

The late sixteenth and early seventeenth centuries saw a proliferation of portraits of fashionable young Isfahanis. Oversized turbans, round cheeks, and sumptuous silk jackets, trousers or cloaks characterize these figures. Often their precise identities are unknown, but in general they were the sons of the Safavid elite, sometimes native Iranians, sometimes *ghulam*s (slaves converted to Islam). Many of these young men were employed in the palaces of the king or his grandees in various domestic capacities including serving at state banquets. The Englishman Thomas Herbert described a reception in 1627 where 'young Ganymedes array'd in cloth of gold with long crisp'd hairs . . . went up and down bearing flagons of gold filled with choice wine'.

In New Julfa, the suburb built to house the Armenian population, Europeans found lodging and Christian churches. Franciscans, Carmelites and other Christian orders were allowed to operate there. Likewise, Shah 'Abbas tolerated Jews and Zoroastrians. While they do not appear to have played as central a role as the Armenians in his economic programme, they did enjoy greater security than they would under the later Safavid shahs. The Armenians lived in Isfahan with a large degree of autonomy and increasing wealth as both foreign and domestic sales of luxury silks grew. In addition to trading, the Armenians farmed silk in the northern province of Mazandaran. Weaving took place throughout Iran, however. The architecture of the Armenians' churches followed prototypes in Armenia itself,

6. Dish, north-west Iran, early 17th century. Glazed stonepaste, diam. 39.7 cm. This dish combines an image of a fashionable Isfahani youth wearing a large turban and feather with Chinese-inspired decorative panels in the border around him.

while their decoration combined Safavid ornament with Christian iconography. Likewise, ritual implements and gospel books used in Isfahan relate stylistically to those employed in Armenia and, with the exception of textiles, show no debt to Safavid Iran.

The women who appear in portraits by leading seventeenth-century Safavid artists fall into two categories: those who are fully clothed and those who are not. The former are rarely identified, but it would appear that they were connected to high-ranking officials through birth or marriage. The latter were most certainly prostitutes, who operated within the law and paid taxes. (In the later seventeenth century, when prostitution was outlawed, contemporary sources remarked on the loss of tax revenue.) Although women at the Safavid court lived in the harem, they were traditionally influential in the choice of the heir to the throne at times of weak leadership. All of Shah 'Abbas's successors were reared in the harem, which resulted in an expansion of the power of the mothers and favourite wives of the shahs, as well as that of the eunuchs who controlled communication between the harem and the outside world.

7. Youth holding a cup, Isfahan, *c.*1600. Opaque watercolour on paper, 14.2 × 7.4 cm.
During the late 16th and 17th centuries, images of young men were produced in large numbers for inclusion in picture albums. Their identities are rarely revealed, which may indicate that they were idealized representations rather than actual portraits.

Following pages
8. Shah 'Abbas and Wali Khan Uzbek at a reception (detail), Isfahan, Chihil Sutun palace, completed 1647.
This wall painting depicts a reception held by Shah 'Abbas for an Uzbek prince, Wali Khan, who was seeking aid against his enemies. The detail shows the sumptuous gold-ground textiles worn by the shah and some of his servants and the palatial setting including wall niches to hold gold bottles.

9. Hookah base, Mashhad, *c*.1610–30. Glazed stonepaste, h. 13.6 cm.
While the blue-and-white glaze and vegetal decoration of this water-pipe
base depend on Chinese models, the figure reclining on a cushion in a tree
reflects the influence of earlier Persian painting. Smoking tobacco became
a popular leisure activity in the early 17th century.

**10. Ceramic ewer with
19th-century metal
spout, Mashhad, dated
1025/1616. Glazed
stonepaste,
h. 24.8 cm, diam. 18 cm.**
The shape of this ewer
derives from Indian
metalwork, whereas its
decoration is based on
Chinese blue-and-white
porcelains. Mahmud Mi'mar
(the 'architect') Yazdi, who
made the ewer, may be
the same man whom Shah
'Abbas commissioned to
renovate the Shrine of
Imam Riza at Mashhad.

11. Flask, Iran, *c.*1590. Brass, h. 37.8 cm.
At the court of Shah ʿAbbas, metal vessels used for pouring
wine and water or lidded bowls for hot food were made of gold
and silver. Analogous objects made of base metal have survived,
but the precious-metal examples have long since disappeared.

**12. Armenian woman
and her child with a
man from Bukhara,
from the Engelbert
Kaempfer Album,
Isfahan, 1684–5. Opaque
watercolour on paper,
page 21.4 × 29.9 cm.**
The German doctor Engelbert
Kaempfer commissioned an
album of paintings of figures
and animals common to Iran,
which he visited in the 1680s.
Here an Armenian woman is
depicted with her face veiled
while a man from Bukhara
offers her a piece of fruit.

13. Censer, Isfahan, 1626. Bronze, approx. h. 11 cm.
The shape and decoration of this censer, made for the Armenian
Christians of Isfahan, reflect a tradition that derives from Byzantine
and medieval Armenian metalwork. The frieze of figures on the
walls of the censer probably represents scenes from the life of Christ.

14. Iranian in a European hat, Isfahan, *c*.1640. Opaque watercolour and ink on paper, 16.8 × 8.6 cm.
During the first half of the 17th century, Europeans visited and lived in Isfahan, providing new sources of visual imagery both from the printed books and images they brought with them and from their own novel clothing and hairstyles. By the mid-17th century, fashionable Iranians sometimes sported European hats while continuing to wear Iranian jackets and trousers.

15. Woman with a ewer, Isfahan, *c.*1630. Opaque watercolour, gold and ink on paper, image 16 × 7.3 cm. Respectable Safavid women appear in portraits fully clothed, often with veils covering their hair. This painting is stylistically very close to works by the Safavid court artist Riza-yi 'Abbasi (see p. 79), who remained active until his death in 1635.

16. Woman giving her dog a drink, signed by Mir Afzal Tuni, Isfahan, c.1640. Opaque watercolour, gold and ink on paper, 11.7 × 15.9 cm.

The seductive pose and dress rolled up to expose this woman's belly and underpants leave little doubt that she is a prostitute. The small dog drinking from a porcelain bowl may have been considered amusing to Safavid viewers, since lap dogs were a European import.

had failed, he left for Europe as the shah's ambassador charged with promoting the anti-Ottoman cause and trade in Iranian silk. Dressed in extravagant Safavid robes and turban, Robert Sherley cut an exotic figure in the capitals of Europe, where he was a walking advertisement for the expertise of Iranian silk-weavers.

In the last decade of his rule, Shah 'Abbas succeeded in taking control of the trade route through the Persian Gulf. Since the early sixteenth century, the island of Hormuz, which lies in the straits of the same name, had been held by the Portuguese, who controlled and taxed all maritime trade entering and leaving the Gulf. In the early 1620s Shah 'Abbas started testing the Portuguese defences. In 1623, with the help of the English, his troops stormed the fort. The attack was successful, and the Iranians henceforth were masters of their entire coastline.

18. The embassy of Khan 'Alam to the Safavid court, India, possibly Kashmir, 18th century. Opaque watercolour and gold on paper, image 29.3 × 17.5 cm. The fame of the Mughal embassy sent in 1613 to the court of Shah 'Abbas lasted in India long after the Safavid dynasty had ended, thanks to the numerous copies of the original image by Bishn Das. The artist who made this version added some figures and musicians to the original composition.

19. Silver crown, England, period of Charles I, 1625–6. Diam. 4.4 cm.
One of Shah 'Abbas's aims in expanding trade with Europe was to increase the amount of silver and gold coming into Iran. This was melted down and used for Safavid coins as well as for silver wire employed in making luxury textiles.

Right

20. Silk brocade (detail), Iran, first quarter of the 17th century. Silk, silver and gold thread with silk core, 186.4 × 86.8 cm.
This textile with its generous lotus blossoms on a ground of silver typifies the luxury silks produced during the reign of Shah 'Abbas. So valuable were they that they replaced other precious items such as Chinese porcelains as appropriate gifts to Shi'i shrines.

23. Sir Robert Sherley, by Anthony Van Dyck, Rome, 1622.
Ink on paper, 19.9 x 15.7 cm.

In 1622 Robert Sherley was in Rome as Shah 'Abbas's ambassador to the Vatican.
His visit coincided with that of the renowned Dutch artist Anthony Van Dyck, who
must have found Sherley's Safavid costume exotic and worthy of his artistic attention.
In addition to this and other sketches of Sherley, Van Dyck painted a life-sized
portrait of Sherley and his wife.

24. The Portuguese defending the fort at Hormuz, from a *Jarunnameh* of Qadri, Iran, Isfahan, 1687. Bound manuscript, image: opaque watercolour and ink on paper, page 29.2 × 19.7 cm. In 1623 the Iranians, with British help, successfully stormed the Portuguese fort at Hormuz in the Persian Gulf. The Portuguese had levied tax on maritime trade in the Gulf for over a century, but now the Safavids gained control of the sea passages that circumvented the overland routes through Ottoman territory.

26. Men loading bales onto a camel, Isfahan, *c.*1630. Ink and watercolour on paper, 11 × 13.5 cm.
In 17th-century Iran, caravans transported goods, internally and internationally. In order to ensure
the smooth flow of trade through Iran, Shah 'Abbas improved the roads and built caravanserais (inns)
at regular intervals along them.

26. Ewer, Iran, dated 1011/1602–3. Brass, h. 32.5 cm.
The shape of this metal ewer derives from an Indian model.
As this indicates, trade with India in the period of Shah 'Abbas
consisted of a broad range of goods. Some of these were copied by
Iranians who modified the decoration to adhere to Safavid norms.

27. Engraving of the maidan with tents, by Corneille le Brun, 1718.
Printed book, double page 20.7 × 36.7 cm.
The maidan of Isfahan continued to serve many purposes until the end of the Safavid
dynasty. Here, many tents have been erected, presumably by travellers or traders.
At other times, elaborate mock battles or firework displays were held in the square.

28. Shrine of Imam Riza, Mashhad.

As the only shrine in Iran where a Shi'i Imam is buried, the Shrine of Imam Riza has retained its prime importance to this day. Shah 'Abbas restored the dome over the Imam's tomb and reorganized the space and water provision to accommodate more pilgrims.

SUFIS AND PILGRIMS

When Shah 'Abbas came to power, the Ottoman empire extended through Syria, Jordan and Iraq to the Arabian Peninsula. As a result, all of the holiest sites in Islam – namely Mecca, Medina and Jerusalem – were in enemy territory. Performing the *hajj*, or pilgrimage to Mecca, is required of all Muslims, but the Ottoman occupation increased the difficulty and risk for Safavids fulfilling this obligation. In addition, Iraq contained the holiest Shi'i shrines: the burial places of Imam 'Ali at Najaf and of Imam Husayn at Karbala. To encourage piety and provide an alternative to the shrines and holy sites that were so difficult to visit, Shah 'Abbas promoted the Shrine of Imam Riza at Mashhad, the burial place of the Eighth Shi'i Imam.

Shortly after the accession of Shah 'Abbas, the Uzbeks seized Mashhad, stormed the shrine, murdered its attendants and stole everything in its treasury. They also looted the solid-gold tiles from the dome over the tomb of the Imam and reportedly defiled the remains of Shah Tahmasp, who was buried there. This destruction and spoliation of the tomb of an important Safavid ancestor posed severe threats to the authority of the newly crowned shah. His opportunity to avenge the loss finally came in 1598, following the death of the Uzbek sultan. The shah's troops regained Mashhad, and he went on to win back Herat and the rest of Khurasan. To express his gratitude, he walked barefoot and bareheaded from the outskirts of Mashhad to the shrine of Imam Riza, where he prayed at the Imam's tomb for success in battle.

Three years later, in 1601, as a sign of his continuing devotion to Imam Riza, Shah 'Abbas completed a 965-kilometre pilgrimage from Isfahan to Mashhad on foot. Once he reached the shrine, he performed humble acts such as sweeping the floors of the Imam's tomb. He spent several months in Mashhad assessing the damage of the earlier Uzbek occupation, ordering repairs to the fabric of the shrine and planning new construction. His particular aims were to ease the congestion resulting from increased numbers of pilgrims and to provide a ready source of water.

In 1608, when Shah 'Abbas donated his porcelains, jades, Persian poetical and historical manuscripts, carpets and other precious items to the dynastic shrine of the Safavids, that of Shaykh Safi at Ardabil, he ordered the conversion of one of its tomb chambers into a Chini-khaneh, or 'China House'. The upper walls were lined with niches whose openings mimicked the shapes of the porcelain vessels. Below these were shelves to receive the manuscripts. Previously, rooms with similar niches to accommodate porcelains and other valuables had been features of palaces accessible only to people from the highest social levels. Now the dervishes who visited the Ardabil Shrine could see the porcelains and even use them; paintings from about 1615 to about 1650 depict groups of dervishes drinking from blue-and-white bowls and jars. What had once been treasures of the Safavid court now acquired a new audience and new users.

29. Old pilgrim, Isfahan, late 16th to early 17th century. Ink and colour on paper, 9.7 × 5 cm. Numerous drawings of aged figures like this one suggest a new awareness of and participation in pilgrimage in the period of Shah 'Abbas.

**30. Illuminated
frontispiece of the
Bustan of Saʿdi, Herat,
late 15th century.
Opaque watercolour
and gold on paper,
page 22.7 × 15 cm.**
Illuminated frontispieces
and chapter headings
appear in the earliest
Islamic manuscripts
and continue as
important features
until the introduction
of printing in the
nineteenth century.
Here the overlapping
geometric design in the
field (central area of
each page) is typical
of late Timurid
illumination. The style
carried over into the
16th century but
disappeared in the
reign of Shah ʿAbbas.

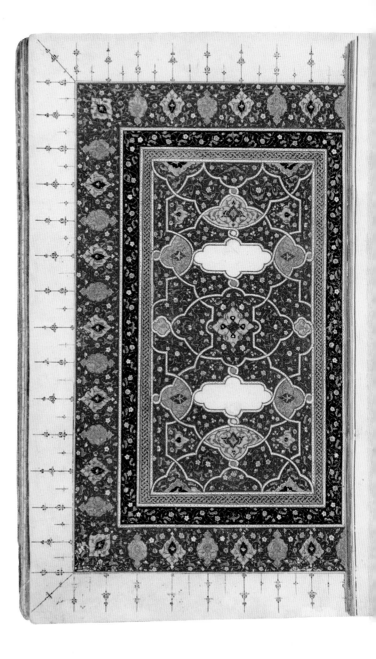

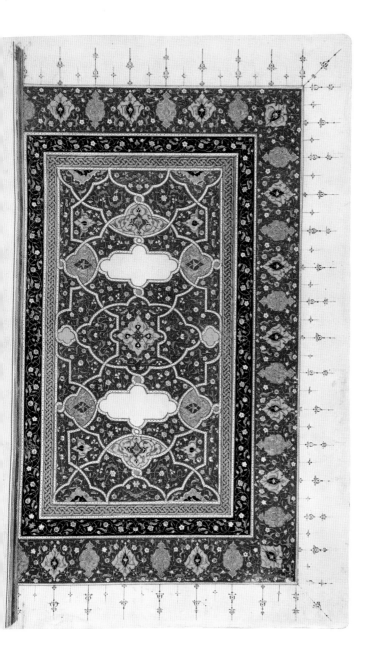

59

**31. Page from a
De Materia Medica of
Dioscorides,
Baghdad, 621/1224.
Opaque watercolour
and ink on paper,
32.8 × 24.3 cm.**
Among the scientific
manuscripts donated
by Shah 'Abbas to
the Shrine of
Imam Riza, was a
12th-century copy
of *Khawass al-Ashjar*,
'The Properties of
Plants', by Dioscorides.
Considered the
foundation of Arabic
pharmacology,
Dioscorides'
De Materia Medica was
disseminated widely
throughout the Islamic
world. This painting
from a dispersed
copy of his text
depicts two doctors
administering
medicine to a very
reluctant patient.

32. Pillar torch stand, Iran, late 16th to early 17th century. Brass, h. 45 cm, diam of base 20.5 cm. Until the 1530s candlesticks with truncated conical bases supplied most of the lighting for large interior spaces, such as the prayer halls of mosques. Pillar-shaped torch stands were introduced during the reign of Shah Tahmasp (1524–76) and remained popular during the rest of the 16th century. This example is missing its top, which would have taken the form of a domed cap that could be turned over and used as the receptacle for lamp oil.

Left

33. Shrine of Shaykh Safi al-Din, Ardabil. This shrine grew up around the tomb of the founder of the Safavid dynasty, Shaykh Safi al-Din. The assemblage of buildings consisted of halls for prayer and rituals as well as tombs of family members. Shah 'Abbas renovated parts of the shrine to emphasize his genealogy going back to Imam 'Ali.

34. Prayer rug, Iran, late 16th to early 17th century. Wool and silk with precious-metal thread, 162 x 104 cm. The design of prayer rugs is closely allied with their use. The central field forms a niche like that of the mihrab, or prayer niche, in a mosque. The mihrab is set into the *qibla* wall, which indicates the direction of prayer for the Muslim faithful, towards Mecca.

35. Shaykh Safi dances to the esoteric words of Shamsa al-Din Tuti, from the *Tazkireh of Shaykh Safi al-Din Ishaq Ardabili*, **Shiraz, Shaʿban 990/August– September 1582. Opaque watercolour, ink and gold on paper, bound manuscript, 35.2 × 22 cm.**

Although this illustration was painted more than three hundred years after the death of Shaykh Safi, it is probably an accurate depiction of Sufi ritual at the Ardabil Shrine. Dancing to the esoteric words of a Sufi master was intended to produce an ecstatic state and help the believer approach oneness with God.

36. Dervish with horn and begging bowl, Isfahan or Qazvin, early 17th century. Opaque watercolour and gold on paper, page 23.5 × 15.2 cm, image 11 × 6.4 cm. Although Shah 'Abbas suppressed some dervish orders who threatened the stability of his reign or preached heretical ideas, the numerous paintings of dervishes from the late 16th and early 17th centuries suggest that such figures were a commonplace sight in Iran at this time. The figure carries a begging bowl and large horn, which were both attributes of wandering dervishes.

37. Large rectangular wine flask, China, Jingdezhen, Jiangxi province, Yuan dynasty, *c.*1330–50. Glazed porcelain, h. 36.2 cm, diam. 25.5 cm, depth 10 cm. Shah 'Abbas presented more than a thousand pieces of Chinese porcelain to the Shrine of Shaykh Safi in Ardabil. Dating from the 14th to 16th centuries, these porcelains were considered objects of great value, thus underscoring the prestige of Shah 'Abbas's charitable donation to his ancestral shrine.

38. Tapestry-woven carpet, Kashan, early 17th century. Silk with precious-metal thread, 301 × 128 cm. In addition to porcelain and manuscripts, Shah 'Abbas donated carpets to the Shrine of Shaykh Safi. This carpet is woven in the tapestry technique, which was quite rare in the Safavid period, making it a fitting gift for the shah's ancestral shrine.

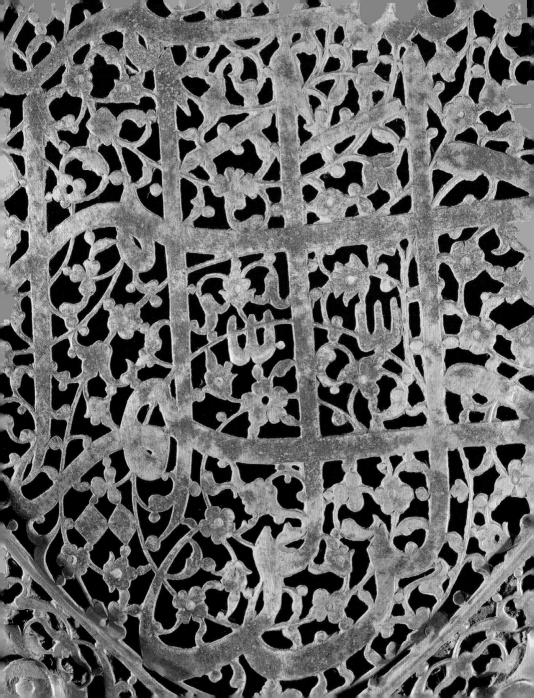

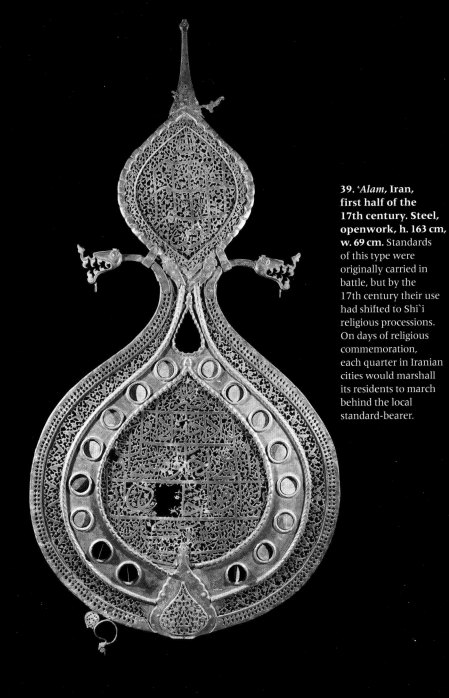

39. 'Alam, Iran, first half of the 17th century. Steel, openwork, h. 163 cm, w. 69 cm. Standards of this type were originally carried in battle, but by the 17th century their use had shifted to Shi`i religious processions. On days of religious commemoration, each quarter in Iranian cities would marshall its residents to march behind the local standard-bearer.

40. Fragment of a tomb cover (detail), Iran, first quarter of the 17th century. Silk brocade with gold threads, 174.1 × 88.5 cm.
Tomb covers were produced to replace ones that had worn out, due either to their age or to being touched by worshippers. As luxury silk production expanded during the reign of Shah 'Abbas, such fabrics were given both to replace textiles that had utilitarian functions at shrines and as charitable donations.

41. Silver mosque lamp, Ardabil, dated 1023/1614. Sheet silver, h. with chain 77 cm, diam. 18.4 cm.
To accompany the opulent gold door and silver grating, twelve silver and gold lamps hung from the entrance to the tomb of Shaykh Safi. The only silver lamp to survive is dated 1614 and is inscribed with the name Sahib Nazir 'Ali Khan, a superintendent of the shrine, indicating that not all the furnishings were contributed by the shah.

ROYAL ARTISTS AND THE NEW STYLE

One of the ways in which Shah 'Abbas sought to impose his will on Iran was by promoting changes in the visual landscape. As with reforms to the legal system, he relied on a small circle of people he trusted to transform the style of Safavid ornament. Tilework swathed the buildings he constructed, carpets covered the floors, silk textiles served as furnishing fabrics and clothing, and illuminated headings marked the opening pages of manuscripts. This profusion of ornament provided the opportunity in a range of settings and situations for a recognizable decorative style to be repeated and refined. Unlike in Europe, where the image of a monarch would appear on coinage and in sculpture in public places, the only portraits of Shah 'Abbas were either produced by non-Iranian artists or for privately owned albums. Calligraphy, by contrast, was used on coins and buildings, where his name and titles were prominently displayed. Traditionally, thanks to its use in all settings, both secular and religious, calligraphy was accorded the highest status among the arts of the Islamic world.

The favourite calligrapher of Shah 'Abbas was 'Ali Riza 'Abbasi, who was appointed head of the royal library in 1598. Although he first trained to design inscriptions for buildings, 'Ali Riza 'Abbasi became equally well known for writing single-page samples of poetry in *nasta'liq*, or 'hanging' script. His versatility and devotion to the shah, whom he accompanied on all of his travels, ensured that 'Ali Riza 'Abbasi was involved in designing inscriptions for the two mosques on the maidan in Isfahan, as well as for the dome of the

42. Four lines of poetry from an album, fol.1b, signed by 'Ali Riza 'Abbasi, Isfahan, dated 1018/1609–10. Ink, opaque watercolour and gold on paper, page 31.2 × 21 cm with borders.
'Ali Riza 'Abbasi, the director of Shah 'Abbas's library, was also one of the king's constant companions. In addition to the monumental inscriptions that he designed for religious buildings, he penned large numbers of single-page calligraphies.

Shrine of Imam Riza at Mashhad. In addition to his own work, he would have directed the staff of the royal library and most likely was instrumental in approving the widespread use of certain decorative devices such as large lotus blossoms, split-palmette leaves, and vase and escutcheon forms that appear in tile-work, carpet design and manuscript illumination.

The leading painter at the court of Shah 'Abbas, Riza-yi 'Abbasi led the development of the Isfahan school of painting in the early seventeenth century. Not only was the palette of primary colours of the Qazvin school replaced by one featuring warm russet, maroon and acid green, but the figural type also changed. Instead of the slim figures of the 1570s to 1590s, men and women with wide, almond-shaped eyes, very round cheeks and heavy, melon-shaped thighs predominate from about 1610 onwards. These figures wear the fabled silk and gold garments produced in Iran and sold to Europeans, Indians and Iranians alike. In the work of Riza-yi 'Abbasi we can observe the birth and development of a new fashion that extended beyond clothes to include facial and other physical characteristics. In our image-conscious age we are accustomed to such changes; likewise, the arts of the period of Shah 'Abbas reveal the omnipresence of fashion and its importance as a marker of identity and modernity.

43. A scribe, inscribed 'Riza drew it', Isfahan, _c._1600. Ink and opaque watercolour on tinted paper, page 15.75 × 12.4 cm, image 10 × 7 cm. This work by Riza-yi 'Abbasi depicts an anonymous scribe. Riza would have worked with the best-known calligraphers employed at the Safavid court to copy books and single pages of poetry, and to design monumental inscriptions.

44. Youth reading, signed by Riza-yi 'Abbasi, Isfahan, *c*.1625–6. Opaque watercolour, gold and ink on paper, page 21.9 × 14.7 cm, image 14.5 × 8 cm. The inscription at the top of this portrait states that it was produced 'on the order of the … Highness', without mentioning the shah's name. The youth wears a cloak made of silk and gold fabric with a design very similar to a surviving textile example (see **20**).

**45. Young dandy,
signed by Mir
[Muhammad] Yusuf,
Isfahan, c.1640–45.
Opaque watercolour
and gold on paper,
17 × 10.5 cm.**
By the 1640s, exposure
to European styles
had led to figures
combining Iranian silk
trousers and cloaks
with European hats.

46. Dish decorated with a sinewy three-clawed dragon pursuing a flaming pearl, China, Jingdezhen, Jaiangxi province, Yuan dynasty, *c.* **1320–50. Glazed porcelain, h. 6.6 cm, diam. 46cm.** Chinese dishes decorated with white slip on a monochrome ground are very rare. They were probably unknown to Iranian potters before Shah ʿAbbas gave this example to the Ardabil Shrine.

47. Ceramic dish, Kirman, second quarter of the 17th century. Glazed stonepaste, diam. 47 cm. Once the Chinese porcelains given to the Ardabil Shrine by Shah 'Abbas were placed on view at Ardabil, they seem to have stimulated new styles of Iranian ceramics, including monochrome wares with slip-painted designs such as this dish.

Preceding pages

48. Chini-khaneh, Ardabil.

In 1611 the ceramics and manuscripts that Shah 'Abbas donated to the Shrine of Shaykh Safi at Ardabil went on view in this newly renovated space. While the niches would have held some of the porcelains, others would have been too large to fit into them and would have been stored elsewhere.

49. Iraqi entertainers with a performing goat, from the Kaempfer Album, Isfahan, 1684–5. Opaque watercolour and ink on paper, 29.9 × 21.4 cm.

The maidan in Isfahan attracted all manner of entertainers, storytellers and others providing or seeking amusement. Although these entertainers are described as 'Iraqi', his term referred to the population of western Iran as well as modern Iraq.

50. Thirty-Three-Arch Bridge, Isfahan, c.1600.
Commissioned by Allahvirdi Khan, one of Shah 'Abbas's most powerful generals and regional governors, this bridge joins the Chahar Bagh – the new palatial district constructed in the 17th century – with the gardens to the south of the Zayandeh Rud river.

Following pages
51. Interior of the dome, Mosque of Shaykh Lutfallah, Isfahan, 1603–19.
The prayer hall of this mosque consists of a single octagonal domed chamber. The warm yellow tiles serve as a foil for the repeating rows of ogives that rise towards the apex of the dome, ever decreasing in size and thus making the dome seem larger than it is.

**52. Collection of
*ghazal*s, Mashhad,
dated 958/1551.
Opaque
watercolour, ink
and gold on paper,
23.6 × 14.8 cm.**
This collection of
*ghazal*s, or love poems,
was copied in elegant
nasta'liq script by Shah
Mahmud Nishapuri,
one of the leading
calligraphers at the
court of Shah Tahmasp.
Nasta'liq, or hanging
script, was the
preferred calligraphic
style for copying
poetry. Shah Mahmud's
sure, crisp letters
characterize this page.
During his lifetime
he enjoyed a good
reputation as a poet,
and it seems that some
if not all of the verses
in this collection were
composed as well as
copied by him.

FURTHER READING

Abisaab, Rula Jurdi, *Converting Persia: Religion and Power in the Safavid Empire* (I.B. Tauris, London, 2004)

Babaie, S., *Isfahan and its Palaces: Statecraft, Shi'ism and the Architecture of conviviality in Early Modern Iran* (Edinburgh University Press, Edinburgh, 2008)

Babaie, S., Babayan, K., Baghdiantz-McCabe, I., Farhad, M., *Slaves of the Shah* (I.B. Tauris, London, 2004)

Blow, D. *Shah 'Abbas, the Ruthless King Who Became an Iranian Legend* (I.B. Tauris, London, 2009)

Calmard, J., ed., *Etudes Safavides* (Paris-Tehran, 1993)

Canby, S.R., *The Golden Age of Persian Art, 1501–1722* (British Museum Press, London, 1999)

Canby, S.R., *The Rebellious Reformer: The Paintings and Drawings of Riza-yi 'Abbasi of Isfahan* (Azimuth Editions, London, 1996)

Canby, S.R., ed., *Safavid Art and Architecture* (British Museum Press, London, 2002)

Crowe, Y., *Persia and China: Safavid Blue and White Ceramics in the Victoria and Albert Museum, 1501–1738* (La Borie, 2002)

Floor, Willem, *The Persian Textile Industry in Historical Perspective 1500–1925* (L'Harmattan, Paris, 1999)

Jackson, P. and Lockhart, L., *The Cambridge History of Iran 6: The Timurid and Safavid Periods* (Cambridge University Press, Cambridge, 1986)

Matthee, R., *The Politics of Trade in Safavid Iran: Silk for Silver 1600–1730* (Cambridge University Press, Cambridge, 1999)

Melikian-Chirvani, A.S., *Le Chant du Monde: L'Art de l'Iran Safavide 1501–1736* (Musée du Louvre Editions, Paris, 2007)

Melville, C., ed., *Safavid Persia: The History and Politics of an Islamic Society* (I.B. Tauris, London and New York, 1996)

Newman, A.J., *Safavid Iran: Rebirth of a Persian Empire* (I.B. Tauris, London, 2006)

Sims, Eleanor, *Peerless Images: Persian Painting and its Sources* (Yale University Press, New Haven and London, 2002)

Thompson, Jon, *Silk: 13th to 18th centuries, Treasures from the Museum of Islamic Art, Qatar* (The National Council for Culture, Arts and Heritage, Doha, 2004)

Welch, A., *Shah 'Abbas and the Arts of Isfahan* (The Asia Society, New York, 1973)

ILLUSTRATION ACKNOWLEDGEMENTS